BRIAN PAUL
PhD, FR

MEDIEVAL ROADS

SHIRE ARCHAEOLOGY

To C.E.

Cover illustration

Part of the Gough map, drawn about 1360, showing south-east England. East is at the top, and London is the prominent town with roads radiating from it in all directions.

Published by
SHIRE PUBLICATIONS LTD
Cromwell House, Church Street, Princes Risborough,
Aylesbury, Bucks, HP 17 9AJ, UK.

Series Editor: James Dyer

ISBN 0 85263 600 8

First published 1982

Set in 12 on 11 point Times roman and printed in Great Britain by C. I. Thomas & Sons (Haverfordwest) Ltd, Merlins Bridge, Haverfordwest.

Contents

Acknowledgements

The author is grateful to Richard W. Bagshawe, who wrote *Roman Roads* in this series, for his thoughts on the roads of a later era; he also provided a number of photographs. The Committee for Aerial Photography at the University of Cambridge were equally helpful in sorting through their massive collection for photographs of possible medieval roads. The maps were designed and drawn from the author's rough sketches by Gustav Dobrzynski of the Department of Geography, University of Salford, and the manuscript typed from the author's even rougher draft by Marie Partington and Moira Armitt of the same department; the author gratefully acknowledges their help.

Plates 1 to 9 and 19 are reproduced by permission of the Committee for Aerial Archaeology, University of Cambridge; plates 10, 11, 13 and 16 were taken by Richard W. Bagshawe, plate 12 by John Steane, Oxford City and County Museum, and the remainder (except plate 14) by the author.

List of illustrations

1
Introduction

The medieval period in England saw a massive growth in all sections of economic life; population increased, towns grew, industry blossomed and trade, which was both a cause and an effect of this growth, became vitally important. Not only was agricultural produce such as grain and wool moved from field to market but also such diverse items as stone, metal, wood, woollen cloth and a whole range of industrial products needed transporting. However, this growth of the whole economy was not continuous; probably beginning with the political stability after 1066 under William I, it tended to stagnate in times of civil unrest such as the reigns of Stephen (1135-54) and John (1199-1216), but certain periods stand out as having more rapid growth, notably the century after John's reign. A period of stagnation followed the poor harvests of 1315-16, and this was made much worse by the arrival of the Black Death in 1348, which seems to have reduced the population by forty per cent in forty years. A long and painfully slow recovery period followed, and it was not until the accession of the Tudors in 1485 that real growth recommenced. This marked the beginning of the end of the medieval period, which finally ended in 1536-40 with the dissolution of the monasteries, which had maintained the medieval way of life, particularly in the more remote areas of northern and western England.

Such was the political and economic background to medieval England. Although relatively few people needed to travel it was vitally important for the whole economy that it was possible for both people and produce to travel easily when required. There were clearly two alternatives: goods could travel by boat or by road. Bulky produce in particular tended to be moved by river or by sea, but most parts of England and Wales did not have this option, as they had no navigable rivers or had rivers that were obstructed by low bridges, weirs or fish traps.

Thus roads must have formed the backbone of the transport system. And yet it is curious that so little has been written about these roads which were so fundamental to England's economic growth. Writers on this topic have largely confined themselves to looking at travellers, road maintenance, the means and safety of travel and the state of the roads. There has been little or no attempt to see *where* the roads were, that is, to view the roads as an integrated network. The reason for this is probably the lack of information available, for virtually no new roads were constructed during this period, and it is very difficult to ascribe a date to a road which was not actually built, but which just came into use. C. T. Flower, writing in 1923, coined the memorable phrase that these roads which grew from habitual lines of travel 'made and maintained themselves'.

There was already a road system in existence, the eight or ten thousand miles (13,000 to 16,000 km) of Roman roads, built mainly by AD 150, but which had not been maintained for well over six hundred years by the time of the Norman Conquest. As we shall see, many of these roads remained in use, providing a basic network. But many of the new towns of medieval England, such as Oxford, Coventry or Plymouth, were not on Roman roads and so new roads must have been needed to serve them, as well as the myriad villages in between.

The nature of these new medieval roads differed from that of Roman or modern roads; essentially the road was not a physical entity, a thin strip of land with definite boundaries; rather it was a right of way, with both legal and customary status, leading from one village or town to the next. If the route was much frequented it became a physical track, but with two important provisos. The first was that if the road was obstructed or had become 'foundrous' in wet weather, then the traveller had the right to diverge from the road, even if that entailed trampling crops; this was even enshrined in law in the Statute of Winchester in 1285. The second proviso was that where the road had to climb a hill or bank then multiple tracks would develop, the traveller taking the easiest route then available. Most of the surviving sections of medieval roads come in this category — where roads left cultivated land and the tracks have thus not been ploughed out or otherwise destroyed. Several of the plates at the end the book illustrate this clearly (plates 1-6).

A few new roads were built; in 1278 Roger Mortimer was charged by Edward I to enlarge and widen the roads and passes into parts of North Wales, clearly in connection with the campaigns against the Welsh. The three causeways connecting Ely with the rest of England across the Fenlands are perhaps the largest medieval road building works, but the earliest charters do not refer specifically to the actual construction of these causeways and there is the faint possibility that they too could be of Roman origin.

Several royal statutes of various dates made requirements about the width of roads and of the land to be cleared on either side − but often more in the interests of safety from outlaws than of improving the roads. The four great highways (Watling Street, Ermine Street, Fosse Way and Icknield Way) were always regarded as being under the kings' special protection, which supports the idea that the Roman roads remained in use in the medieval period.

The greatest problem in attempting to trace medieval roads is that if the route is no longer in use then, not having been engineered, it will largely have disappeared. On the other hand, if it has remained in use it will have had a more modern road constructed on top, burying or destroying any archaeological evidence of the medieval road. In order to trace medieval roads, therefore, one must begin in the library rather than in the field. As we shall see, there is written evidence in the form of medieval maps, travellers' records, place-names and so forth which can help us to see which Roman roads remained in use and where medieval roads came into use. All this evidence will help us to link together the widely scattered and difficult to date archaeological remains. This book must thus devote a good deal of attention to the sources of information on medieval roads rather than concentrating on the often dubious physical remains, for virtually the only way to confirm field evidence of a medieval road is to demonstrate from the historical record that it was in use during that period. A medieval road may have originally come into use in pre-Roman, Roman, Saxon or medieval times, but we must have evidence for its use between say 1066 and 1485; when it first came into being is of little importance.

2
Travel in medieval times

Medieval travellers

It used to be thought that few people travelled out of their own town or village in medieval times; certainly people as a whole travelled far less than they do today, but the notion of a peasant or villein spending the whole of his life in one place is not typical. At the start of the medieval period, with the imposition of the feudal system, villeins were not free to leave their manor permanently, though they would doubtless know their local market town well. After the Black Death had reduced the population, because of the shortage of labour and other socio-economic changes men started to move to find better paid work; these paid workers were outside the feudal system, which was by then in rapid decline.

J. J. Jusserand in his classic book *English Wayfaring Life in the Middle Ages* devotes most of his attention to various travellers, both lay and religious. In addition to workmen he includes minstrels, messengers, merchants and outlaws in his first category and preachers, friars, pardoners and pilgrims in the second. He could also have included travelling justices, sheriffs, revenue collectors and two rather special types of traveller, bishops and kings, who are special because it is possible to trace their actual movements, often on a day-to-day basis.

In particular, the itineraries for the kings, which were compiled from letters they wrote, charters they granted or simply from the details of their household accounts, are the most useful, for from the time of King John onwards we have an almost complete record of each king's whereabouts. More than that, the entire court was itinerant and moved with the king, certainly until well into the fourteenth century. Thus the baggage train, comprising from ten to twenty carts and wagons, containing everything from the treasury to the king's wardrobe, had to move about with the king and must have required adequate roads. The kings were almost constantly on the move and we hear few complaints about the condition of the roads.

Certain types of trade on the road led to some roads being given special names, such as Maltways, Oxdroves, Sheepdroves and, above all, the Saltways. These roads were not specifically constructed for these uses but were named after the type of traffic which frequented them. The roads leading from the inland salt towns (wiches), including

Droitwich, Nantwich, Middlewich and Northwich, are well known, and their courses can usually be traced by 'salt' place-names such as Saltersford, Saltersgate and the like.

Other place-names can give clues to old routes; *way* is probably the commonest, but *stretton, heol, fford* and *gate* can all refer to a road, coming from Latin, Welsh, Welsh and Danish respectively. Any word having a connection with roads derived from any of these languages can suggest the line of a former road. We shall see how place-name elements can be used as collaborative evidence in the study of a local area later in the book.

A more bizarre type of road was that known as a *corpse road.* In many parts of England, particularly in the more remote areas, the establishment of churches did not keep pace with the growth of population. Thus enormous parishes survived, and although there were usually several subsidiary chapels in these large parishes, only the parish church would have had the right of burial, and consequently the dead had to be carried there to be buried. The parish of Kendal (Cumbria) was such a parish; it extended to include not only what is now Bowness-on-Windermere but also Ambleside and Grasmere over 16 miles (25 km) from the parish church. Perhaps the large number of deaths by plague in 1348-9 hastened the creation of new parishes of Grasmere and Windermere in those years. Corpse roads sometimes carried little other traffic in remote areas; the villagers of the now flooded village of Mardale Green (Haweswater) took their dead some 6 miles (10 km) over Mardale Common and down Swindale for burial at Shap. Old Ordnance Survey maps show another corpse road running across Burnmoor from Boot-in-Eskdale to Wasdale Head.

Conditions on the roads

Opinion has long been divided on the state of the roads in medieval England. One school of thought dwells largely on the difficulties of travel, noting that in wet weather the roads became rivers and that in winter they became impassable for wheeled traffic. Indeed Parliament was postponed in 1339 because so many members were held up by the bad weather. On the other hand there is strong evidence that the haulage of heavy goods was undertaken in autumn and winter. For example, stone was transported over 6 miles (10 km) to build Vale Royal Abbey (Cheshire) with the carters making two round trips every day for a month at a time, even in winter; the slack months were May, August and September.

As we have already seen, the best information on medieval travellers is contained in the royal itineraries and these can also be used to see whether travel in the winter was difficult. The kings had to move to collect taxes and to consume dues in kind, and the earlier medieval kings in particular were constantly on the move. King John spent only one month of his entire reign without a move, and that was when he was besieging Rochester Castle in November 1215. He moved, on average, over twelve times each month throughout his reign, moving constantly throughout the year, though travelling least in June and October (fig. 1).

Edward I was also a great traveller, concerning himself much with affairs in Wales and later in Scotland. He averaged almost nine moves each month throughout his reign, favouring August and September, and travelling least in November (fig. 2). In January 1300 he covered the 360 miles (575 km) from Bamburgh to Windsor in twenty-five days including six days when he did not travel. He was thus averaging about 20 miles (32 km) a day; clearly travel in winter presented few problems to the movement of the royal household. The king and his retinue with their horses, wagons and carts represented a not unusual type of traffic on medieval roads. Travel, although slow, was something undertaken as a matter of course, even in winter.

By the end of the medieval period the roads were still in a tolerable condition; John Leland, travelling around 1540, rarely complains of them, but William Harrison, writing in 1586, says that the highways had deteriorated drastically in the previous twenty years. There are two possible causes for this change; the first was the dissolution of the monasteries in 1536-40, for they had effected much of what little road maintenance was done, and the second was the rapid growth of the Tudor economy. In medieval times the roads had been generally adequate both in quantity and quality for the amount of traffic using them. In the mid sixteenth century it seems that the fine balance between the ability of the roads to maintain themselves and the amount of traffic was upset, and it was only then that the roads became unable to cope with the sheer volume of that traffic.

3

Archaeological evidence

Whereas our knowledge of the Roman road system has always been based principally on archaeological evidence, the fact that medieval roads were not formally constructed or engineered makes any such line of investigation of them difficult. What remains of the field evidence is of two kinds: tracks and bridges. Tracks sometimes remain intact, especially where the land has not been ploughed. Even where tracks have gone across farmland they can often still be seen on aerial photographs, either as actual tracks or as crop marks (plate 8). On the ground the most impressive feature is the *holloway* or sunken road, found when a road descended a slope and became virtually a stream channel in times of heavy rain, thus deepening the road often to a depth of 10-20 feet (3-6 m) (plates 20 and 21). For the rest, the field archaeologist has to be content with raised or sunken tracks across fields, or double lynchet ways where a track was cut into a slope or hillside. It is rare to find a stretch of track more than a mile in length, and most are much shorter, leaving us with a host of disjointed local tracks, many of which may not have been in use in medieval times. One always has to return to the documentary sources to see whether any particular road was in use in medieval times.

Deserted medieval villages are perhaps the one large-scale exception to this rule, for in such cases part of the medieval landscape has been fossilised, and old routes which are no longer used can be identified. Plate 9 shows the village of More in Shropshire, which was created out of the neighbouring parish of Lydham in the early twelfth century. It was a defended village, being close to the Welsh border and in a valley which must often have seen Welsh invasions. The village thus had a motte and a ringwork, but clear traces of house platforms and roads can still be seen today both from the air and on the ground. The village decayed to its present size of a church and a handful of houses only in the sixteenth century, so in this case at least we can be very certain about the date of the abandoned road.

Bridges and causeways, however, attracted more attention than roads in medieval times. Their provision and maintenance was regarded as a pious act, and consequently church records often refer to them. Special taxes *(pontages)* were sometimes raised for their upkeep, and they figure more often than roads in medieval court cases. Medieval bridges were simple at first, being wide enough only for packhorses; there was usually a ford alongside for wagons. Stone bridges are numerous, the earliest being about 1180; they include a thirteenth-century one at Castle Combe (Wiltshire), and the one *c* 1500 at Sutton (Bedfordshire) (plate 13). Even in remote north Westmorland (now part of Cumbria), twelve stone bridges are known to have existed in the fourteenth century.

A few towns had fortified bridges; examples still survive at Warkworth (Northumberland) and Monmouth (Gwent) (plates 14-15); such large bridges were needed in many places, especially near towns and on the major routes such as the bridges at Staines and Windsor on the main road west from London or on the Welsh border road as at Ludlow. Here the whole development of the town was altered when new streets were laid out and a new bridge built. The town grew originally between the castle, which is on a rocky promontory above the river, and the main north-south route through the Marches; this junction (the Bull Ring) formed one end of a large market area, now much infilled (fig. 3). The town grew around the market area and on either side of the north-south route (Corve Street and Old Street), until a large extension to the town was laid out in the thirteenth century and the traffic was diverted through the market and down Broad Street to the new bridge over the river Teme. The road to Hereford, south of the river, may also have been diverted some distance to the west, although its earlier course is uncertain.

Perhaps the best known example of where a new bridge altered the course of a road as well as the fortunes of a whole town is where the Great North Road crosses the Ure (fig. 4). Formerly the Roman road crossed near what is now Aldborough (North Yorkshire), but the building of a new bridge in the early twelfth century shifted the route half a mile (800 m) to the west, and the new town of Boroughbridge grew up there. The road which used to lead from Aldborough to the river Ure degenerated into a grassy lane and finally ceased to be a road altogether when the village was enclosed in 1809.

Some causeways were quite substantial; Holland Bridge near Boston (Lincolnshire) was 10 feet (3 m) broad and 8 feet (2.4 m) high, having thirty bridges in one section. Maud Heath's causeway, which runs for $4\frac{1}{2}$ miles (7 km) near Chippenham (Wiltshire), was built as a legacy in 1474 to enable people to cross the river Avon dry-shod. However, if the Fen Causeways to Ely are medieval, then they are clearly the largest examples in England.

4
Documentary evidence

Documentary evidence is sparse and often of a negative kind, such as the references to impassable roads in court cases. Roads or their ditches were frequently blocked; for example, in 1357 the Fosse Way was obstructed with trenches, piles and trees at Belgrave (Leicestershire). In 1386 the Abbot of Chertsey allowed two 'wells' 12 feet (3.7 m) wide and 8 feet (2.4 m) deep to exist in the high road from Egham to Staines; an unknown man had drowned and the abbot had claimed his goods! Local enterprise in Norfolk must have been somewhat discouraged when a man was fined for building a new road from Yarmouth to Winterton to replace one blocked with sand.

The scattered references to roads in medieval documents are important in that these specific roads are thus known to have been in use. For example, Holm Cultram Abbey (Cumbria) had a right of way 'by the ordinary road through Bassenthwaite' from 1290 to 1327, and the Roman road from Kendal to Shap is referred to as *magna strata, magna via* and *stayngate* (paved road) at various times during the medieval period. In 1354 Bishop Welton promised forty days of remitted penance for anyone working on a boggy stretch of road at Wragmyre between Carlisle and Penrith. It is unusual for a road (rather than a bridge) to be the subject of such an indulgence.

Further south, an inquest in Suffolk in 1364 requested the Lord of Bildeston to clean two ditches on the road to Nedging, and in 1285 Edward I wrote to the Prior of Dunstable ordering him to repair the high roads through Dunstable, probably Watling Street and the Icknield Way:

Writ

Edward, by grace of God, to his beloved in Christ the Prior of Dunstable and the burgesses of the same vill, greeting. Because we have learnt that the high roads, which stretch through the middle of your vill aforesaid, are so broken up and deep by the frequent passage of carts, that dangerous injuries continuously threaten those passing by those roads: we wishing to be guarded against such injuries, which by that fault will be able to happen in the future unless the remedy be more speedily applied, command you that you, that is to say, each one of you according to his estate and capabilities, shall cause those roads to be filled in and mended, as in such case it has been accustomed to be done in times past. So that for default of you in this part it shall not be necessary for us to

apply a heavier hand to this. Myself being witness at Westminster, the 13th day of February in the fourteenth year of our reign.
Annales Prioratus de Dunstaple in *Annales Monastici (1866)* translated by K. C. Newton.

There are numerous such references to roads, but it is usually difficult to find records for any specific road.

Chaucer's *The Canterbury Tales,* published in 1400, is a set of stories woven around a pilgrimage from Southwark to Canterbury; he makes no mention of the route or the state of the roads and mentions only five places on the way. Perhaps we can assume that the route was well known and presented no difficulty to travel.

The movement of bulky produce has left few records and it was only when the government became involved with such trade that records have survived. In particular, records were kept for the provisioning of the kings' armies; the accounts give details of the goods bought or requisitioned, and the type of transport used to take the goods to the customs ports for shipment to Wales, Scotland or France. The best surviving records are those for Lincolnshire and Yorkshire; here goods were moved to progressively larger centres, eventually by river, though it should be remembered that these two counties are well served by rivers – which does not apply to most of England. Records also survive for the various Cistercian monasteries which moved their wool to distant ports chiefly by packhorse or cart. Such long hauls as those from Furness Abbey (Cumbria) to Beverley (Humberside), Holm Cultram (Cumbria) to Newcastle, and Vale Royal (Cheshire) to London or Boston (Lincolnshire) suggest that these long distances were not unduly difficult. The detailed routes, however, are not known.

Itineraries

The various itineraries of the medieval period, whether compiled at the time or posthumously, provide direct evidence of the movement of individual people, rather than the simple physical existence of roads. There is, for example, the itinerary of Giraldus Cambrensis, who toured Wales in 1188 with Archbishop Baldwin, and a great many bishops' itineraries survive from the mid thirteenth century onwards. Unfortunately the bishops visited only a few places, and detail is usually lacking. Occasionally records of the movements of private individuals were kept; the best known is the route recorded by Robert of Nottingham, who was buying wheat for the king in 1324-5 in the area around the river Trent.

The most complete itineraries, however, are those compiled for the kings; as we have already seen, they were itinerant and would visit a wide range of places, from castles to manors and abbeys to market towns. Problems arise in the interpretation of these itineraries, principally where information is lacking, but once the routes are plotted on a map it is reasonable to suppose that if a king (and his court) used certain routes frequently, then some reasonable track or road must have existed. The routes taken by John, Edwards I and Edward II are shown in figs. 5, 6 and 7. In each case there are two maps, the first showing all the routes travelled, and the second showing only those travelled three times or more.

King John (fig. 5) was noted even in his own time as a great traveller; he carried his scrutiny into the far north and west where kings seldom went – indeed his visit to Carlisle in February 1201 was the first time that any king had been to that area since William II wrested the land from the Scots in 1092. John was probably too efficient an administrator for his time (his predecessor, Richard I, had spent only six months of his ten-year reign in England), and although many state records start during his reign and we can therefore trace his movements accurately, this efficiency no doubt helped his ultimate downfall. Sometimes there are enormous gaps in his itinerary, such as on his second visit to Carlisle in 1206, when he is last recorded in the city on 20th February and next appears in Chester on 1st March. It is impossible to say which route he took; on fig. 5 the route is shown via Kendal and Lancaster, though he could equally well have gone by sea! Happily there are few gaps of this magnitude.

Edward I's itinerary (fig. 6) shows twice as many journeys as that for John; in particular he travelled to Wales and Scotland – his routes beyond the Scottish border are not shown on the maps. Perhaps the most curious aspect of his travels is how little he used the same routes, suggesting, if nothing else, that cross-country travel presented few problems. Edward II (fig. 7) also covered very few routes more than twice. In particular his route to the north stands out clearly: it ran along Watling Street to King's Langley and Stony Stratford, and then diverged to Northampton, Leicester, Nottingham, Doncaster, Pontefract, York, Northallerton, Darlington, Durham and Newcastle to Berwick. In addition Edward certainly seems to have travelled by boat on the Trent and the Ouse; he could equally have used the Thames but his mode of transport is impossible to ascertain from the itinerary.

An attempt has been made to condense these maps into one which shows all the routes travelled four times or more by more than one of the three kings (fig. 8). Clearly they travelled mostly in central and southern England, avoiding Wales (apart from Edward I), the north-west, the south-west and, perhaps more surprisingly, East Anglia, an area of great economic importance. Perhaps the later monarchs remembered the loss of King John's baggage train in the silt of the Wash after leaving King's Lynn in October 1216 (plate 11).

5
Map evidence

If the archaeological and documentary evidence is poor and uneven, we are fortunate in having several medieval maps showing roads on a national scale. Matthew Paris, a monk at St Albans, drew four maps of Britain in about 1250 which are based on an itinerary from Dover to Newcastle (fig. 9). The route forms the backbone of the maps and it goes by way of Canterbury, Rochester, London, St Albans, Dunstable, Northampton, Leicester, Belvoir (a cell of St Albans), Newark, Blyth, Doncaster, Pontefract, Boroughbridge, Northallerton and Durham. On map C the route continues north to Berwick and on map D the route has Leicester on a branch route, the main route going via Stamford, and Newcastle is not shown (fig. 10). Only on map D, which is in any case only an unfinished sketch, are the towns actually connected by lines. Paris probably derived the route from a written itinerary and tried to fill in the rest of the country around it. The maps are crude and must be used with caution, for a legend on map D disarmingly states that the island would have been elongated if the page size had been larger!

Much better evidence for the road system, however, is to be found on the Gough map of about 1360, which depicts some 2,940 miles (4,730 km) of roads covering most of England. Part of the map appears on the cover of this book, and Cumbria is shown in fig. 11. It is not known who drew the map; it is named after the antiquarian, Richard Gough, who first described it in 1780. Interpretation of this map is made difficult because neither its purpose nor its sources are known, but it appears to have been an official compilation for government use, perhaps amended for use in certain areas – for example the extant copy has networks of local roads in south-east Yorkshire and Lincolnshire. Distances are given between most towns, probably in old French miles (about $1\frac{1}{4}$ statute miles or 2 km) and almost forty per cent of the routes shown are along the line of Roman roads.

Gough map: roads and distances
Main roads and branches

M1 London X Kingston V Cobham XV Guildford IX Farnham VII Alton VII Alresford VII Winchester XX Salisbury XVIII Shaftesbury XII Sherborne XX Crewkerne XII Chard XI Honiton XII Exeter XX Okehampton XVI

(Launceston) XX . . . Camelford XV Bodmin . . . St Columb X . . . V St Ives

M2   London . . . Brentford XVII Colnbrook VII Maidenhead X Reading XV Newbury VII Hungerford VIII Marlborough XXX Chippenham XX Bristol

M2a   Reading XX Oxford

M3   London XV Uxbridge XII High Wycombe X Tetsworth X Oxford X Witney VII Burford VIII Northleach XV Gloucester VII Newent XVII Hereford XII Clyro X Brecon X Llywel XVIII Langadock . . . Llandeilo X Carmarthen . . . St Clears XI Llawhaden VIII Haverfordwest VII St Davids

M3a   Oxford XII Faringdon XX Malmesbury XX Bristol

M3b   Oxford V Abingdon

M4   London X Barnet X St Albans X Dunstable VIII Stratford . . . Buckingham VI Towcester XII Daventry XVI Coventry VIII Coleshill XII Lichfield . . . Stone VI Newcastle-under-Lyme XXIII Warrington VIII Wigan XII Preston XX Lancaster XVI Kendal XX Shap . . . Penrith XVI Carlisle

M4a   Stratford V Northampton XII Market Harborough XII Leicester

M4b   Stone . . . Stafford

M5   London XII Waltham Abbey VIII Ware XIII Royston IX Caxton VIII Huntingdon XIIII Ogerston V Wansford V Stamford XVI Grantham X Newark X Tuxford X Blyth VIII Doncaster X Pontefract XX Wetherby VIII Boroughbridge XIIII Leeming X Gilling X Bowes XIIII Brough XI Appleby X Penrith

M5a   Ware XII Barkway XII Cambridge X Newmarket X Bury St Edmunds X Thetford XXXII Norwich

M5b   Doncaster XIII Wakefield . . . Bradford . . . Skipton X Settle XII Kirkby Lonsdale VIII Kendal

M5c   Kirkby Lonsdale . . . Shap

Secondary roads and branches

S1   Southampton . . . Havant XXII Chichester X Arundel X Bramber X Lewes XVIII Boreham Street . . . Battle VII Winchelsea VIII Rye . . . Appledore XVII Canterbury

S2   Cardigan XXIII Aberystwyth XII Aberdovey XII Barmouth XI Llaneddwyn . . . Harlech XII Criccieth XXIIII Caernarvon VIII Bangor XV (Capel Curig) VIII Conwy . . . Abergele IIII Rhuddlan X Flint X Chester

S3   Bristol XV Newport XV Gloucester VIII Tewkesbury XIII Worcester X Droitwich XIIII Solihull VIII Coventry XVI Leicester X Melton Mowbray X Grantham

S3a   Droitwich X Birmingham X Lichfield XVI Derby XV Chesterfield XVI Doncaster

S3b   Worcester XII Kidderminster XII Bridgnorth XV Shrewsbury XII Ellesmere VII Overton XII Chester X Liverpool

S4   Bristol X(V?)

S5   Bristol XIII Axbridge

S6   Richmond X Bolton X Hawes X Sedbergh X Kirkby Lonsdale

S7   Bridport X Lyme

Local roads – Lincolnshire

L1   Lincoln XIIII Sleaford

L2   Lincoln XXVI Boston

L3   Lincoln X Spital-in-the-Street X Kirton . . . Brigg VIII Barton

L4   Barton XII Caistor XVI Horncastle V Bolingbroke IX Boston

L5   Boston XII Spalding

L6   Boston XII Wainfleet

Local roads – Yorkshire

Y1   Leeming XII Helperby X York

Y2   York XIIII Malton V Pickering

Y3   York X Pocklington VII Market Weighton

Y4   York XVI Market Weighton VIII Beverley

Y5   York XVI Howden

Y6   Beverley XVI Bridlington XII Scarborough XII Whitby
      XVII Guisborough

The map omits several well known roads such as those from
London to Dover and York to Newcastle, although it does show the
towns *en route* correctly. The omission of the latter route is a particular puzzle, as it was much used as the main route to Scotland.
Viewing the map as a whole, the sheer number of towns shown would
enable the traveller to plan a journey, even if an actual route was not
shown. Many places such as Bitchfield (between Stamford and Lincoln) and Bentham (between Settle and Lancaster) are included only
because they were stages between larger towns. Overall the criteria
for the choice of towns shown on the map remain a total mystery.
The roads do, however, reflect the centralisation of government, for
there is clearly a national road system radiating from London, despite
the fact that certain important towns, such as Plymouth, King's Lynn
and Colchester, which were probably amongst the ten largest in size,
are not connected to the network at all. York, the second largest
town, is poorly served, and Lincoln has only local roads, although
from here the normal route to York would have been by river.
    It is tempting to presume that the lines marked on the map
represented actual roads on the ground; they probably did with those
routes which ran along Roman roads, although there are numerous
examples of where later roads have developed alongside Roman
roads, because travellers shunned the hard surface (if it still survived)
for the softer ground alongside. The routes which do not follow
Roman roads must have been tracks which made themselves through
the continual passage of traffic; at worst they were directions on the
map to guide the traveller across open country. The routes of
Matthew Paris and the Gough map are shown on a modern map in
fig. 12.

6
Studies of individual roads

Studies of medieval roads on the small scale have tended to look either at roads within a single parish, usually where an early map survives, or at one particular route, which may have surviving earthworks. In their aerial survey of medieval England, Beresford and St Joseph choose the village of Padbury (Buckinghamshire) to study in some detail, having already looked at its fields and the effects of enclosure. Their starting point is an Elizabethan plan of the parish dated 1591 (fig. 13). This shows a radial network of seven lanes with branches and cross routes, leading from the village street out into the fields. Most of them degenerate into smaller tracks, including the one named 'Buckingham Waye' which led to the county town, less than 3 miles (4.8 km) distant. The other route named as heading for a specific place, 'Whadden Waye', made its way across the fields for almost 6 miles (10 km) to Whaddon, but this route is now only a footpath. Such local roads were of vital importance to the needs of the village; they led out to the fields and to outlying woods, pasture or mills. They were irregular in both direction and width, and few continued even to the parish boundary, let alone to adjoining villages.

In areas of more dispersed settlement, away from the typical compact villages and open fields of midland England, the road network is totally different - with lanes linking one isolated farm to the next, though again there were comparatively few direct routes between villages which were, in any case, far apart. Such patterns are well seen in the south-western counties of England.

Virtually the whole rural landscape of England has been totally altered since medieval times by the enclosure of the open fields. Whereas medieval roads had some degree of freedom to move or spread out, the new enclosure roads were made straighter and were confined by walls or hedges. Unfortunately, few detailed pre-enclosure maps survive, so it is difficult to see how the pattern of roads has changed unless the land has remained largely undisturbed by deep ploughing, thus allowing the medieval field tracks to survive. These can often be seen on aerial photographs, sometimes with the former road network totally separate from the present-day one (plate 9).

Examples of the way in which a medieval road would spread out over a large area are best seen where the road left cultivated land, and in particular where it had to climb a hill and was able to diverge over the common or waste land. Several examples are given in the photographs at the back of this book (plates 1-6), including Rodborough Common near Stroud (Gloucestershire), Walkers Hill near Alton (Wiltshire) and Postern Hill near Marlborough (Wiltshire). In the two plates (1 and 2) showing Twyford Down near Winchester (Hampshire), it is possible to see the road leaving the cultivated land of the Itchen valley as it makes its way south, barely a mile from Winchester, to join a ridgeway to the South Downs, and to link the county town directly with the Bishop's palace at Waltham and the boroughs of Portchester and Portsmouth. The tracks branch out to climb the 200 feet (60 m) of Deacon Hill just below the iron age ramparts of St Catherine's Hill. There is still a modern track climbing the hill directly, but the present road swings round to the east to take the hill more gently.

Plate 3 shows Beacon Hill, about 1½ miles (2 km) east of Amesbury in Wiltshire. Here the London to Bath road descends some 270 feet (80 m) from Beacon Hill, towards the crossing of the river Avon at Bulford. This route has now been rendered obsolete by a newer crossing of the Avon, further south at Amesbury. There are numerous other examples throughout the country, but they are limited in extent and the date of such tracks cannot be known for certain.

Roads were important in determining the success or otherwise of towns and their markets; many of the towns which failed were simply not well located with respect to the road system. At Brough in Cumbria, for example, a castle was built in about 1100 on the site of an old Roman fort (fig. 14). The foundation failed to prosper, however, largely because markets were held further north at Market Brough, which was sited on a medieval diversion of the Roman road descending from Stainmore, on its way to Appleby, Penrith and Carlisle. We have already seen how, in Ludlow, the main road, a river crossing and a planned extension to the town all affected each other.

Studies of individual routes are rare; but C. Taylor has studied several routes in the east Midlands (fig. 15). The first is a study of the road from Stamford (Lincolnshire) to Kettering (Northamptonshire). In this case various subsequent diversions can be seen both in the villages and in the fields *en route*. In particular there is a fine holloway some 6 feet (2 m) deep and 35 feet (11 m) wide south of Bulwick, which runs parallel to the modern road for most of the way to Deenethorpe, where the medieval road runs into the village, and is represented by a holloway once again south of the cul-de-sac in the village.

A short distance to the south-east, in Cambridgeshire, Taylor gives a somewhat more complex example showing the changes in a route from Roman times to the present day, where the Roman road was probably abandoned in favour of drier routes further west, most of which have, in their turn, been abandoned, at least as through routes. The main medieval road from Wansford went by way of Coppingford and Ogerston to Alconbury. Ogerston was a medieval manor and, although a farm is all that remains today, it is marked on the Gough map as the stage between Huntingdon and Wansford. Another medieval route leaves Ermine Street near Sawtry, also trying to avoid the fenlands; each of the villages through which this route passes is laid out along it, even though it is now represented only by a disjointed set of lanes and paths. Finally there is evidence to suggest that the Roman road had come back into use later in the medieval period.

In the Lake District there are fewer complications with Roman roads, as only two major roads crossed the mountain core; one ran from Kendal to Ravenglass via the fort at Hardknott and the other ran along and gave the name to the mountain ridge of High Street. Any fellwalker in the Lakes will be familiar with the zigzag paths which wind their way up most of the passes from Nan Bield in the east to Sty Head in the west. Again it is difficult to date these tracks, but their earliest use is probably medieval, even though they were not causeyed or surfaced in any way until the sixteenth century at the earliest.

As trade increased the elaborate zigzag routes were constructed to ease the gradients of the mountain passes for the packhorses. The modern hiker in his haste normally ignores these, and thus they usually survive. Two good examples can be found close together at the head of Langdale: Stake Pass climbs north towards Borrowdale and Rossett Gill has its packhorse route well away from the steep and stony climb of the gill itself (fig. 16 and plates 17-19). Furness Abbey, situated in the extreme south-west of Cumbria, had lands in upper Eskdale (near Hardknott) and also in Borrowdale some 8 miles (13 km) further north, across some of the highest land in England. One of the passes between them is called Ore Gap, and it was certainly used for the movement of iron ore in medieval times, albeit in small quantities (fig. 16 and plate 19).

There are many books which deal with individual routes at a local or county level — but they all struggle with the problem of dating the roads; three very different examples are those by Barnes, Cochrane and Dodd, all listed in the bibliography.

7

The road network

Very few attempts have yet been made to look beyond individual roads or parishes to try to establish what the medieval road network was like. The present author has made a study of the roads of the medieval diocese of Carlisle, which is fortunate in having the itinerary of Bishop John de Halton (1292-1324) to help in a reconstruction of the road system. Here we shall look at one county, Cheshire, and then tentatively at the whole of England.

Cheshire

While this short study cannot hope to be definitive because of the lack of detailed field evidence, it will show how the various historical sources can be used. The first step is to establish the Roman road network – though the precise route of large sections of it is uncertain – notably the route from Chester to Wilderspool (fig. 17).

Also shown on this map are place-name elements which suggest the existence of a road; they include *ford, bridge, street* and *stretton* and the Welsh elements *cryw* (ford), *ffordd* or *heol* (road) and *sarn* (causeway). These place-names appear again in fig. 18, where, by a process of connecting each one to its nearest neighbour and looking in detail at the alignments of the villages and their roads, it is possible to piece together several 'linear routes', one of which is along the Chester to Wilderspool route. D. Sylvester has also suggested three other routes in the east of the county which have been partly identified in the field. Cheshire was important commercially for its salt production and there are several 'saltways' linking the 'wiches' to various 'salt' place-names.

Saltways were not special roads in any sense, and the far-flung 'salt' place-names are connected by roads known to have been in use either in the medieval period or later. Place-names are only of limited value, principally because they do not give a date to a road and often refer to pre-medieval roads.

More useful are the royal itineraries, and the travels of Edward I and Henry III are plotted in fig. 19. Many of the routes taken by the monarchs follow known roads, but some do not, for example those between Ince and Vale Royal and between Macclesfield and Nantwich. Edward's route to Overton probably went along the route shown in the Gough map. Few of the routes used by the kings follow place-name roads; only those from Nantwich to Combermere and from Barnshaw to Macclesfield do so. The Gough map roads are also shown on this map, including the main road to the north which passes through the county from Newcastle to Warrington, and although two intermediate places are shown, its precise route is uncertain. The other road on the map was from Shrewsbury and divided at Chester to go into North Wales and Liverpool. Again, its route can only be guessed at.

Chester was an important town in medieval England. Although it probably had a population of just over two thousand for most of the period, its lack of growth caused it to fall from being the fourth largest borough in England in 1086 to forty-second largest in 1348. Nevertheless, it would have had strong links and good roads to towns like Shrewsbury, York and London. In such local studies it is also sometimes useful to use post-medieval evidence, but only to confirm the existence of earlier roads. The earliest of such sources usually dates from the sixteenth or seventeenth century, and the roads given by Harrison, Smith, Ogilby and Morden at various dates between 1586 and 1695 are plotted on fig. 20.

A synthesis of all this information, together with much detailed fieldwork, would lead us nearer a true picture of the medieval roads of Cheshire. As it stands, this cartographic approach has left us with many unresolved problems, in particular the routes taken by the Gough map roads and the general confusion around Middlewich and Nantwich. In some areas parallel lines of travel less than a mile apart follow each other over considerable distances, and there appears to be no major route into Wales from the southern half of the county. Nonetheless, the maps show the importance of Chester and the main route from Newcastle-under-Lyme to Warrington. On the other hand the 'wiches' are surprisingly poorly connected, although they are all linked to Chester, which may have been an important distribution centre. A generally flat county such as Cheshire would present few obstacles to travel, which no doubt accounts for much of the proliferation of routes.

This short study of Cheshire has attempted to show how all the sources and methods mentioned earlier can be applied to an area the size of a county and we must hope for more research at this level. It is possible at this scale to build up a broader picture than can be obtained by looking solely at one road.

England and Wales

Any attempt to build a national picture of the road network must be speculative, but there is considerable evidence to show us which were the most important routes. Our starting point must be the Roman road system, large parts of which were clearly still in use, as shown by the Gough map and the royal itineraries, despite the ravages of time and weather since the departure of the Romans. Indeed their routes have persisted, and many are still in use today, though not always as through routes. All this evidence can be brought together to show which Roman roads were still in use in medieval times, and these appear as solid lines in fig. 21. This map also shows the evidence of roads on contemporary maps and the major routes used by the kings which were not along Roman routes, all of which can be truly described as the medieval roads which made and maintained themselves.

This distinction between the two types of road is especially apparent in certain areas; Cirencester is an important junction in the Roman system, yet Oxford and Windsor are totally divorced from it. Other distinctions emerge too; Oxford is an important junction on the map evidence, but the itineraries give more prominence to the palace of Woodstock, 8 miles (13 km) to the north. The principal centre is clearly London, followed, in order, by York, Marlborough, Leicester, Salisbury, Winchester, Woodstock, Lincoln, Chester, Shrewsbury, Lichfield, Gloucester, Oxford and Windsor. This network is clearly at its best in central and southern England, and poor in all the surrounding areas.

8
Tracing medieval roads

Whilst the chief excitement of tracing medieval roads always lies in following their course across the countryside, one first has to do a good deal of vital and significant groundwork in the library. The first step is to obtain an up-to-date, reliable and accurate map of Roman roads in the area you intend to study. The Ordnance Survey's *Map of Roman Britain* certainly does not show all the known or presumed roads, and often recent research has not yet been brought together even at a county scale. Usually you will have to search through local archaeological journals, and the county record office, museum or local history library should be of great help, both with references and with putting you in touch with the local expert on Roman roads.

When one has established the probable Roman road network, the next step is to see how much of it was used in medieval times, and then to see where new roads had come into use. This requires searching through the map evidence, whether it be the Gough map or later local or county maps, and using modern large-scale Ordnance Survey maps (the 6 inches to 1 mile, or 1:10,000 map is ideal) as a base on which to plot all the available information. These maps also show a vast number of place-names, which can reveal old routes. Local charters may mention roads; the local bishop may have granted indulgences to anyone repairing roads or bridges; usually the dates of the building of bridges are known and travellers from the king downwards may have left records. In particular the itinerary of Edward I is well worth consulting.

Your county record office and local history library are the best places to start research. Because of the difficulties of dating a road in the field, it is much better to do all the documentary research first and then move on to look for any physical remains. Air photographs are especially useful and probably the best collection is in the University of Cambridge, whose collection is classified by both subject (for our purpose 'Ancient roads') and by parish; most parishes in England and Wales are covered, and because old tracks show up best from the air, especially with low sunlight, study of aerial photographs is often more rewarding than trying to trace the same feature in the field.

Finally, armed with all the available documentary and cartographic evidence, you can go into the field to see what, if anything, remains of medieval roads, and, above all, to see more clearly what options were open to the traveller in medieval England. There is a vital need for further research at the local and county level to discover exactly what did happen to the roads of England in the twelve hundred years between the departure of the Romans and the building of the first turnpike roads.

9

Select bibliography

Medieval England
Cantor, L. (editor). *The English Medieval Landscape*. 1982.

Roman roads
Bagshawe, R. W. *Roman Roads*. 1979.
Margary, I. D. *Roman Roads in Britain*. 1967.

Medieval roads
Beresford, M. W. and St Joseph, J. K. S. *Medieval England – An Aerial Survey*. 1979.
Flower, C. T. 'Public Works in Medieval Law'. *Seldon Society* 32 and 40. 1915 and 1923.
Gough, H. *Itinerary of King Edward the First*. 1900.
Hindle, B. P. 'The Road Network of Medieval England and Wales'. *Journal of Historical Geography* 2 (1976) 207-21.
Hindle, B. P. 'Seasonal Variations in Travel in Medieval England'. *Journal of Transport History* 4 (1978) 170-8.
Jusserand, J. J. *English Wayfaring Life in the Middle Ages*. 1884.
Martin, G. H. 'Road Travel in the Middle Ages'. *Journal of Transport History* 3 (1976) 159-78.
Stenton, F. M. 'The Road System of Medieval England'. *Economic History Review* 7 (1936) 1-21.

Medieval maps
Hindle, B. P. 'The Towns and Roads of the Gough Map'. *The Manchester Geographer* 1 (1980) 35-49.
Parsons, E. J. S. *The Map of Great Britain c AD 1360, Known as the Gough Map*. 1958.

Local studies
Barnes, B. *Passage through Time – Saddleworth Roads and Trackways*. 1981.
Cochrane, C. *The Lost Roads of Wessex*. 1969.
Dodd, A. E. and E. M. *Peakland Roads and Trackways*. 1980.
Hindle, B. P. *Lakeland Roads*. 1977.
Taylor, C. *Roads and Tracks of Britain*. 1979.

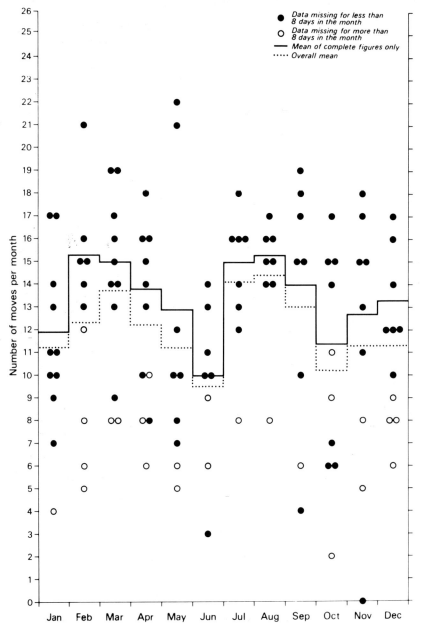

Fig. 1. King John: number of moves per month. Each month of his reign is represented by a circle; for example, in two separate Januaries he moved seventeen times, and in another January he moved only four times, though this last figure is based on incomplete evidence. He moved on average almost twelve times each January throughout his reign.

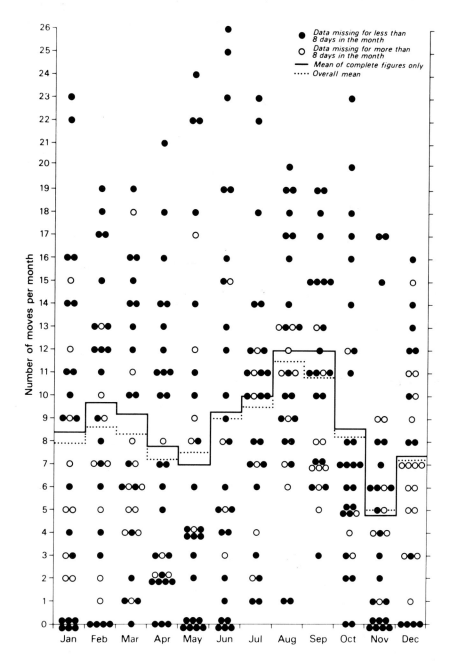

Fig. 2. Edward I: number of moves per month.

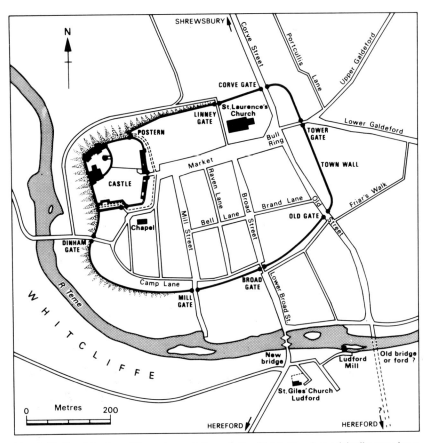

Fig. 3. Medieval Ludlow. The main road through the Welsh Marches originally ran along Corve Street and Old Street but was diverted into the town's market and thence down Broad Street to a new bridge over the Teme.

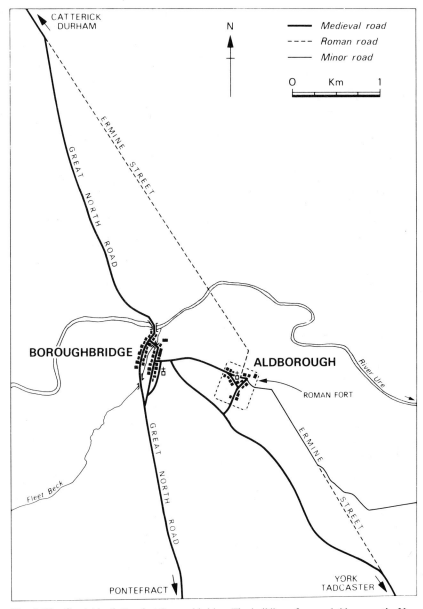

Fig. 4. The Great North Road at Boroughbridge. The building of a new bridge over the Ure resulted in the diversion of the road and the decline of Aldborough.

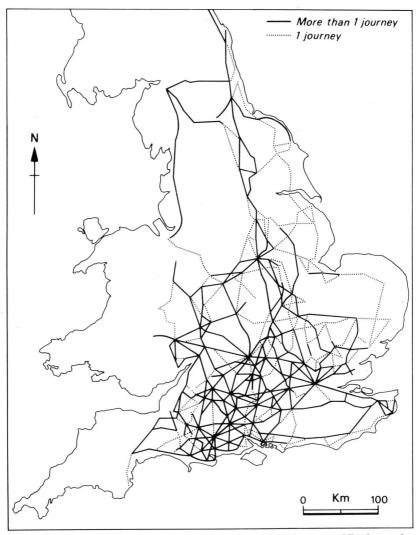

Fig. 5. The itinerary of King John. The map above shows all his journeys, whilst that on the opposite page shows only routes he travelled three times or more.

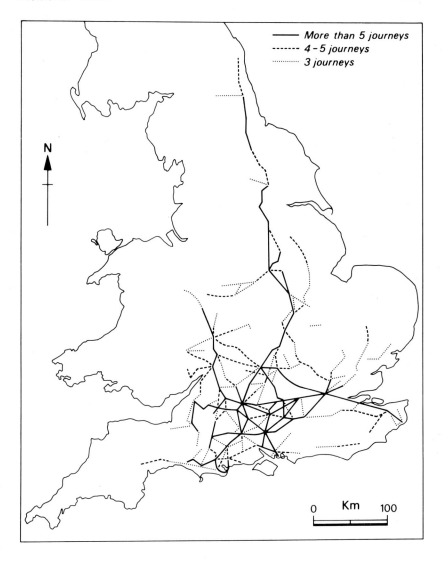

More than 5 journeys
4 – 5 journeys
3 journeys

N

0 Km 100

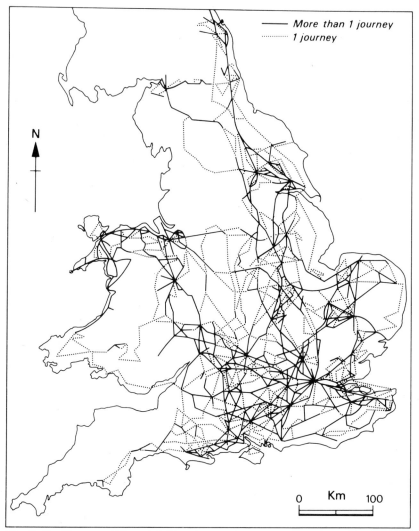

More than 1 journey
1 journey

N

0   Km   100

Fig. 6. The itinerary of Edward I. Note how much he travelled to Wales and Scotland. (Journeys actually in Scotland are not shown.) The map above shows all his journeys, whilst that on the opposite page shows only routes he travelled three times or more.

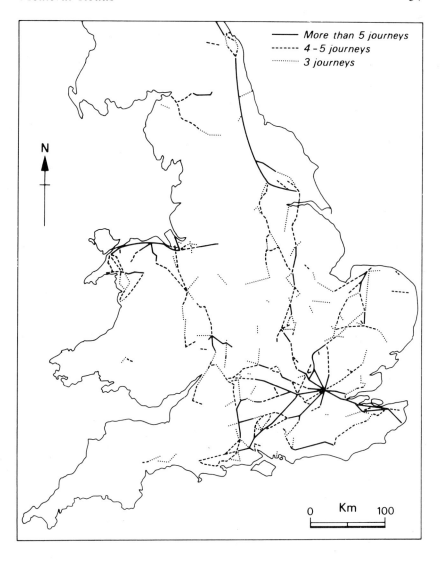

More than 5 journeys
4 - 5 journeys
3 journeys

N

0   Km   100

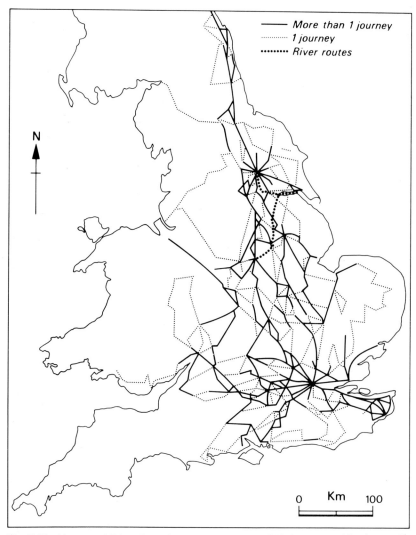

Fig. 7. The itinerary of Edward II. The map above shows all his journeys, whilst that on the opposite page shows only routes he travelled three times or more.

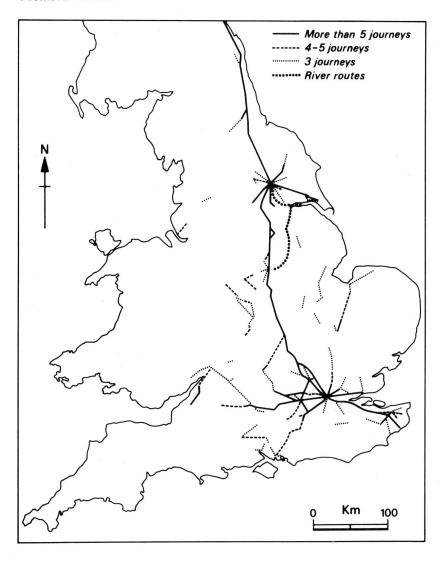

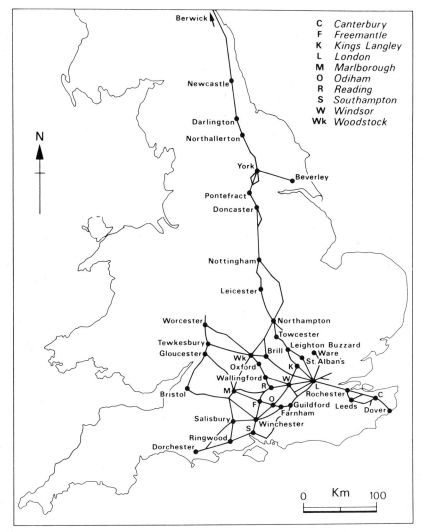

Fig. 8. The royal itinerary network. This map shows a basic route network which would have been used most often by the three kings, John, Edward I and Edward II.

Fig. 9. The Matthew Paris map (version A). This map, drawn in 1250, shows a single route from Dover to Newcastle.

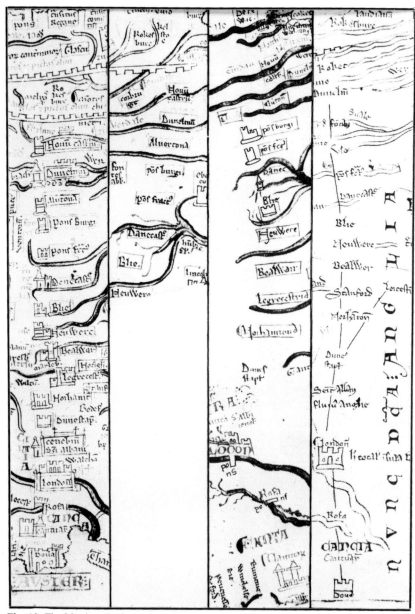

Fig. 10. The Matthew Paris route, as it appears on the four surviving versions of his map.

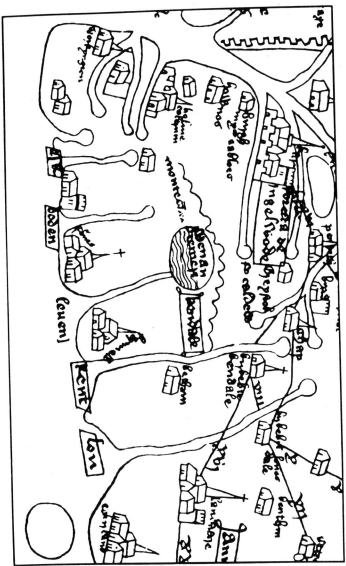

Fig. 11. Cumbria on the Gough map. This map, drawn about 1360, shows roads leading southwards from Carlisle. Another part of the map appears on the cover of this book.

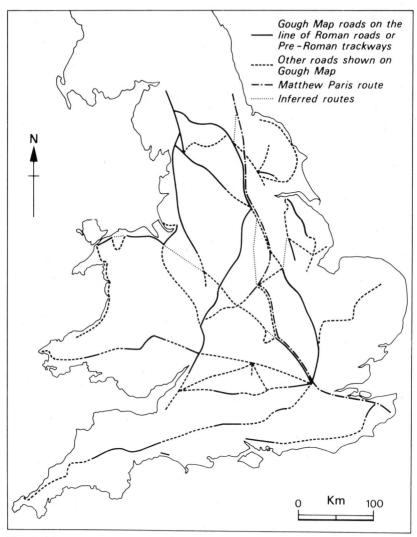

Gough Map roads on the
line of Roman roads or
Pre-Roman trackways

Other roads shown on
Gough Map

Matthew Paris route

Inferred routes

N

0   Km   100

Fig. 12. The routes of the Paris and Gough maps (see also figs. 9-11).

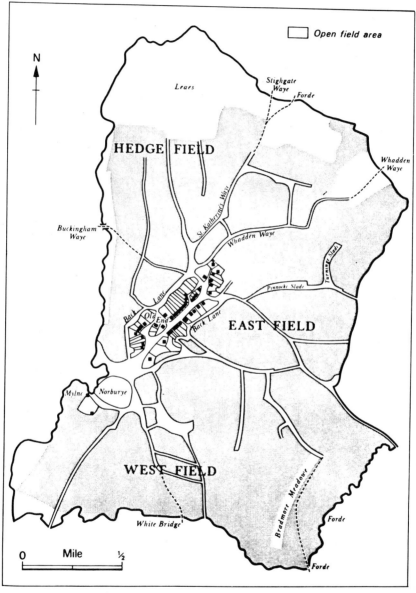

Fig. 13. Medieval Padbury. A plan based on a sixteenth-century map of the village, showing the irregular nature of local roads. (After Beresford and St Joseph.)

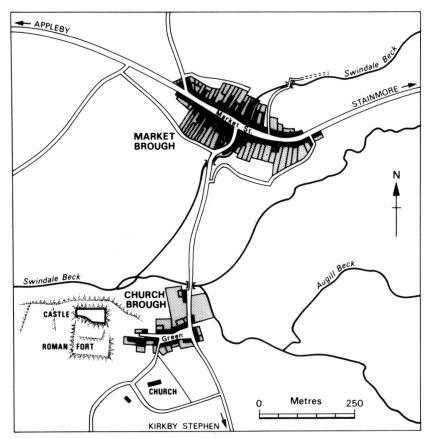

Fig. 14. Medieval Brough. The course of the Roman road is uncertain but it probably lay parallel to the medieval road, though 650 yards (600 m) to the south, coming directly into the Roman fort. The medieval castle built on the site of the fort failed to attract any settlement, as traders preferred the new town of Market Brough on the diverted road.

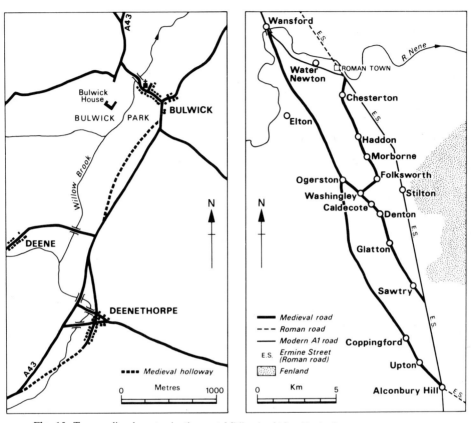

Fig. 15. Two medieval routes in the east Midlands. (After Taylor.)

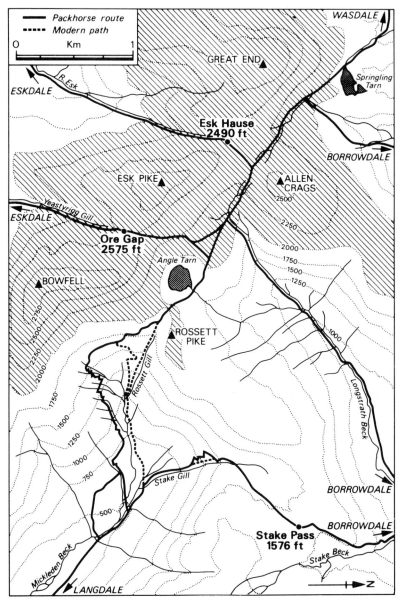

Fig. 16. Rossett Gill, Stake Pass and Ore Gap; showing the original pony tracks and some of the modern short cuts.

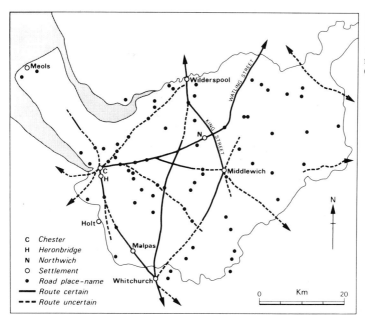

Fig. 17. Roman roads and road place-names in Cheshire.

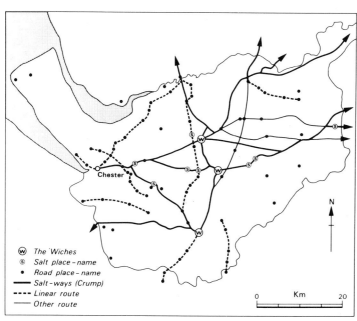

Fig. 18. Medieval routes in Cheshire.

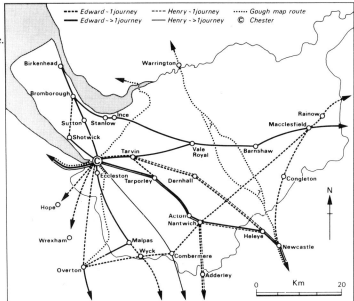

Fig. 19. Royal itineraries in Cheshire.

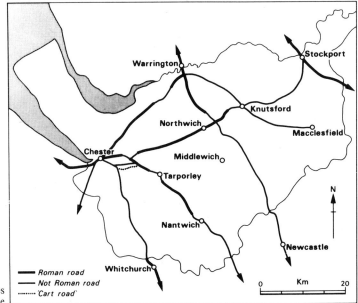

Fig. 20. Post-medieval map routes in Cheshire.

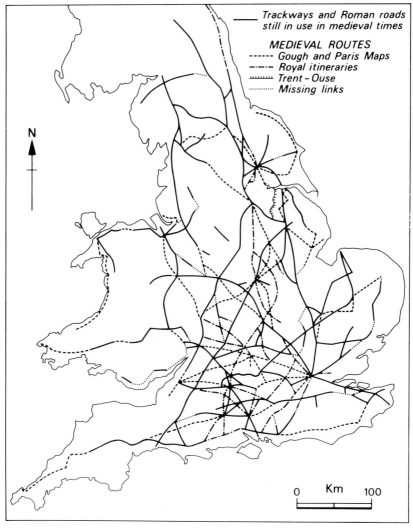

Fig. 21. Medieval routes. All the solid lines are Roman roads and trackways still in use, as opposed to the routes which came into use in medieval times.

Plate 1. Twyford Downs, Hampshire. A vertical aerial photograph showing the multiple tracks created by travellers climbing out of the Itchen valley. The road still in use was a Roman road.

Plate 2. Twyford Downs, Hampshire. An oblique aerial photograph of the same area as plate 1. Generally, old roads and tracks are best observed on oblique photographs.

Plate 3. Bulford, Wiltshire. An aerial view (looking south-east) of the multiple tracks descending from Beacon Hill towards the crossing of the river Avon.

Plate 4. Postern Hill, near Marlborough, Wiltshire (looking south). Numerous tracks climb the hill barely a mile south-east of Marlborough.

Plate 5. Walkers Hill, near Alton Priors, Wiltshire. The multiple tracks climb out of the Vale of Pewsey along the line of a ridgeway, north towards Avebury and Marlborough Downs.
Plate 6. Rodborough Common, Gloucestershire. A fine set of multiple tracks winding their way on to the Cotswolds, immediately south of Stroud.

Plate 7. Winsford, Somerset. Multiple parallel tracks alongside the B3223 across Winsford Hill.

Plate 8. Ampleforth, North Yorkshire. Multiple tracks across a flat field are revealed here as crop marks which would probably not be obvious when viewed from the ground.

Plate 9. More, Shropshire. The deserted medieval village can be seen laid out on either side of an abandoned road running from the motte to the present-day road.
Plate 10. Gaddesden Row, Hertfordshire. A modern road built on the agger of a Roman road which was itself built on a prehistoric ridgeway. A good example of a road probably in continuous use for thousands of years.

Plate 11. Wash Lane, Clenchwarton, Norfolk. An 18 foot (6 m) wide green lane with deepened side ditches. This is the traditional route of King John's baggage train to and from King's Lynn in October 1216.

Plate 12. Newbridge, Oxford. The finest medieval bridge in Oxfordshire, built at the junction of the Windrush and the Thames. Note the humped-back shape, pointed arches and projecting piers (cutwaters).

Plate 13. Sutton Bridge, Bedfordshire. A packhorse bridge (*c* 1500) with a ford alongside.
Plate 14. A nineteenth-century photograph of the defended medieval bridge at Warkworth, Northumberland.

Plate 15. The defended bridge at the south-west entrance to the town of Monmouth, Gwent.

Plate 16. Castleton, Derbyshire. Packhorse trail along Corve Dale near Peveril Castle.

Plate 17. Stake Pass, Langdale, Cumbria. The largest zigzag on the pass, now almost entirely neglected by modern fellwalkers.

Plate 18. Stake Pass, Langdale, Cumbria. The author standing on one of the zigzags which came into use to ease the gradient. The minor engineering and surfacing was not done until at least the sixteenth century.

Plate 19. Rossett Gill and Ore Gap, Cumbria. The old packhorse track A-A-A can just be seen, keeping well clear of the steep and stony bed of the gill. The modern zigzag (B) can also be seen. The route continues to Angle Tarn and Esk Hause and is crossed by the route from Ore Gap (see fig. 16).

Plate 20. Richard's Castle, Herefordshire. A view up the 'holloway' towards the deserted medieval village; the motte and church are above the farmhouse, and the remains of the village in the field to the right.

Plate 21. Richard's Castle, Herefordshire. Looking down the steep hill, the 'holloway' is more obvious; it has cut down some 15 feet (5 m) through shales, which are exposed to the left of the road.

Plate 22. Blackstone Edge, Greater Manchester. One of the finest surviving sections of Roman road in Britain, climbing eastwards across the Pennines from Littleborough. Many such Roman roads were still in use in medieval times.

Plate 23. Blackstone Edge, Greater Manchester; only a few yards from the previous photograph. The Roman road has been almost completely destroyed, yet its route still provides the easiest way across the moorland. In medieval times many Roman roads would have looked like this.

Index